The AIDS Awareness Library

Kids with AIDS

Anna Forbes, MSS

The Rosen Publishing Group's
PowerKids Press
New York

To Arran, 9, and Carl, 7, and all of their generation.
May they live to see the cure.

Published in 1996 by The Rosen Publishing Group, Inc.
29 East 21st Street, New York, NY 10010

First Edition

Book design: Erin McKenna

Photo credits: John Michael/International Stock; p. 4 © Robert C. Burke/Liaison International; p. 7 © Dario Perla/International Stock; pp. 8, 12, 16 by Seth Dinnerman; p. 11 © James Davis/International Stock; p. 15 © George Ancona/International Stock; p. 19 © Dusty Willison/International Stock; p. 20 © Jeff Christensen/Gamma Liaison.

Forbes, Anna, MSS.
    Kids with AIDS / by Anna Forbes.
          p.   cm. — (The AIDS awareness library)
    Includes index.
    Summary: Explains, in simple terms, how AIDS and HIV viruses effect children who are infected and how family and friends can help them.
    ISBN 0-8239-2372-X
    1. AIDS (Disease) in children—Juvenile literature. [1. AIDS (Disease). 2. HIV infections. 3. Diseases.] I. Title. II. Series.
RJ387.A25F67 1996
362.1'98929792—dc20
                                              96-14328
                                                      CIP
                                                       AC

Manufactured in the United States of America

Contents

Kids with AIDS

AIDS has only been around for about 20 years. Half a million people in the United States have it already. Most of them are grown-ups.

About 7,000 kids in the United States have AIDS. About 5,000 of these kids got HIV, the **virus** (VY-rus) that causes AIDS, before they were born. Other kids got HIV from **donated** (DOE-nay-tid) blood or **medicine** (MED-ih-sin) made from donated blood. But now scientists know how to test blood so that no one else can get HIV that way.

◀ Scientists learned how to test blood for HIV.

Living with HIV or AIDS

HIV is the virus that causes AIDS. Someone with HIV may not get AIDS for many years. Most people with HIV try hard to stay healthy. They want to live normal lives for as long as they can. They take medicine, eat well, and get lots of rest.

You may know someone who is living with HIV or AIDS. This book will help you understand how that person lives his or her life.

Most kids with HIV can do the things that kids without HIV do. ▶

Vickie

Most kids who are born with HIV don't get sick for a long time. Vickie is nine years old. She was born with HIV. She and her older brother live with their grandmother. Their mother died of AIDS a few years ago. Her brother doesn't have HIV or AIDS. Vickie misses her mom. But most of the time she's pretty happy. The only time she really thinks about having HIV is when she has to take her medicine. Vickie takes a lot of medicine to help her stay well. But her friends never make fun of her.

◀ Kids with HIV need good friends too.

Jamaal

Jamaal is in sixth grade. He had HIV for 11 years. Now he has AIDS. Jamaal is a little shorter than most of his classmates. He's also very thin. Sometimes he gets sick. Last year, Jamaal was in the hospital for three months.

When he's sick, he likes people to visit him. When he was in the hospital, his teacher brought him his schoolwork. But what he liked best was when his friends came to see him. They brought him snacks and told him what was going on at school.

Kids with AIDS may not be able to play sports or do other things that involve running around. ▶

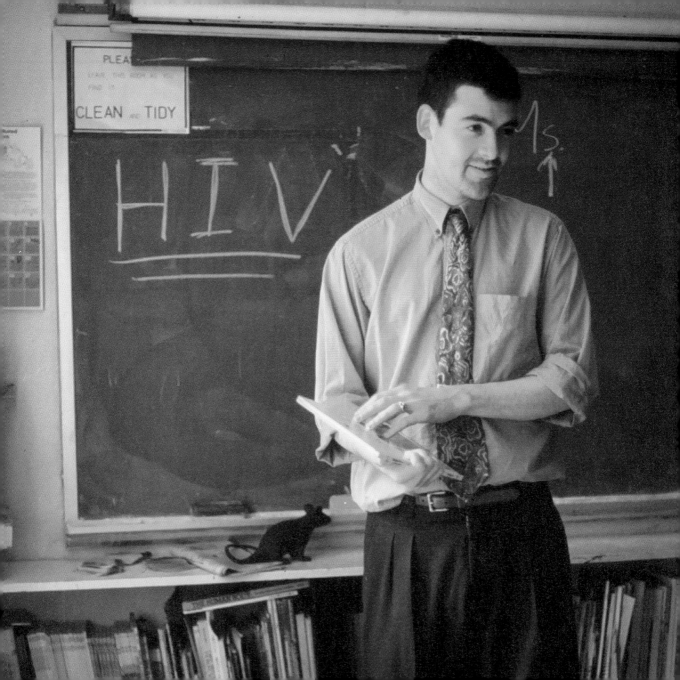

Kids Knowing the Facts

Jamaal and Vickie need people to know the facts about HIV and AIDS. Their teachers talk about HIV and AIDS in class. Students learn that people get HIV and AIDS mostly by having unsafe sex or by sharing a needle to use drugs. They learn that HIV can't travel from one person to another by doing everyday things. It's safe to share food, play games, and sit with people who have HIV. Jamaal and Vickie are lucky because their friends treat them the same as they treat other people.

◀ Teachers can help kids learn more about HIV and AIDS.

Friends Helping Out

Sometimes Jamaal can't eat because the food hurts his stomach. Sometimes he gets really tired even when he's not sick. Then he doesn't feel like playing or running around.

Jamaal's friends know that this is just part of having AIDS. They don't make fun of Jamaal or try to make him do things he doesn't feel like doing. They just help him out by getting a teacher, or by letting him rest.

One way a person can help a friend with AIDS is by doing something he can take part in. ▶

Classmates Helping Out

One day, Vickie's class was reading a story about people with AIDS. During lunch that day, Vickie seemed really sad. Her classmate, Maria, asked Vickie if she was okay. Vickie nodded, but she wouldn't look at Maria. Maria gave her a hug, and said that it was okay to be sad. She asked Vickie to sit with her at lunch. Vickie nodded again, but this time she looked right at Maria and thanked her. By the end of lunch, Vickie felt much better. And Maria had made a new friend.

◀ Sometimes a hug can make all the difference.

Kids Affected by AIDS

Some kids don't have HIV or AIDS, but they are **affected** (ah-FEK-tid) by them anyway. They may have a friend or relative who has HIV or AIDS. These kids may feel sad, angry, or scared. They may stay home to be with the person who is sick. Listening and talking to a friend who is affected by AIDS can help him or her feel better. Doing something together can help take your friend's mind off of AIDS for a while. People who are affected by AIDS really need their friends.

You can help take your friend's mind off of AIDS by doing something fun. ▶

Teaching Others About AIDS

Some kids deal with AIDS by teaching other kids about it. Wearing a small piece of red ribbon tells others that you care about what happens to people with AIDS. One school had a red ribbon project. A teacher brought in red ribbon. Students cut it up and put a pin in each strip. The students sold the red ribbons for 25¢. They raised over $700. They donated the money to an organization that helps people with AIDS. This project got a lot of kids thinking and talking about AIDS.

◀ The red ribbon in support of people with AIDS has become so popular that it's even on a postage stamp.

Dealing with AIDS

It is important to remember that AIDS is a disease, much like chicken pox or measles. You have to be careful not to put yourself at risk for getting the disease. But you don't have to be afraid of someone who has HIV or AIDS. A person who has HIV or AIDS needs friends. Now that you know the facts about HIV and AIDS, you can be a good friend to someone with HIV or AIDS.

Glossary

affected (ah-FEK-tid) Feel the result of something.

donate (DOE-nayt) To give to someone else.

medicine (MED-ih-sin) Something that helps make an illness go away.

virus (VY-rus) Germ that causes disease.

Index